ROBERT A. REID

A QUALITY LIFESTYLE

A 6-step Problem-solving Process for Time-sensitive
Root Cause Analysis, Corrective Action, and
Continuous Improvement.

CREATE
A QUALITY LIFESTYLE

ISBN 978-1-0995339-1-4

Printed in the United States of America.

CONTENTS

CREATE

A QUALITY LIFESTYLE

"CREATE IN ME A CLEAN HEART, O GOD;
AND RENEW A RIGHT SPIRIT WITHIN ME."

~ KING DAVID

PREFACE

If a quality of life is important to you, your family and organization, then establishing a spirit of excellence is critical to achieve your goal. Your ability to properly communicate with people, manage resources, and streamline processes is a valuable skill. Such intention would require the discipline to follow a proven way to resolve problems, mitigate risks and sustain a quality lifestyle.

In the corporate world, the International Organization for Standardization (ISO) is an authoritative body that sets standards for companies to comply with. Third-party entities utilize these standards to conduct audits against companies' practices and procedures for certifications. Companies' compliance to the ISO requirements will ensure safe, reliable, and quality goods and services for consumers and stakeholders.

So ISO is very concern about defective product escaping from companies into the hands of customers. In particular, ISO 9001 standard on Quality Management sets requirements for companies' Quality Management Systems (QMS), their procedures and policies. A section of the company's QMS should address the processing of discrepant or nonconforming materials.

Today, there are many notable continuous improvement methodologies. Companies have developed or adopted unique 'ways' to defining, investigating and solving problems, which cause defects. The continuous efforts of companies to mitigate likely risks and mistake-proof known problems help to sustain their reputation, brand, competitiveness and financial gains.

Here are a few types of methodologies beyond the 'do it now' and 'get it done already' attitudes. The "Plan, Do, Check, Act" cycle as outlined by Walter Shewhart and modified as, "Plan, Do, Study, Act" cycle by W. Edwards Deming formalized the fundamental principles of a problem-solving process. There are also methodologies such as Six Sigma, which use data to reduce process variations of critical customer criteria.

The primary focus of the CREATE Process however, is to provide a 6-step problem-solving process for time-sensitive root cause analysis, corrective action, and continuous improvement for personal and organizational uses. While this CREATE Process is not focused on quantitative analysis or data-driven decisions, it provides a robust way to ensure the problems, complaints or concerns are addressed.

Without further delay, let me say thanks to my peers, trainers, managers, and quality leaders and various personnel whom I have had the honor to work with on Quality projects. Thanks to the Six Sigma Quality Department at General Electric Company, Energy Division. Thanks to the Quality Engineering department at L-3 Communications. Thanks to the Quality Assurance department at Sikorsky, a Lockheed Martin Company. And many thanks also to American Society for Quality (ASQ) and its Body of Knowledge, training, network and certifications in Quality Assurance for its global membership. Your dedication to QUALITY is exceptional!

It is my hope therefore that you will find this book simple and yet interesting to read, and the CREATE Process insightful and useful to address personal and business related problems. As you encounter problems in life, don't stay stuck wondering why things went wrong, or what to do next. Instead, learn this novel approach on how to CREATE A QUALITY LIFESTYLE by applying this 6-step problem-solving process for time-sensitive root cause analysis, corrective action, and continuous improvement.

Thanks, Rob Reid

INTRODUCTION

What's wrong? What's keeping you up at night? What's the one problem you wish could just go away? These are the types of questions I would ask managers and project owners to determine whether a problem was significant enough to be added in the queue of my quality projects.

I have come to realized that living this "Quality Lifestyle" requires having a quality thought-life. In order for you to solve various types of problems you must be willing to learn the ways of process improvement. While a few people are aware of any continuous improvement methods, even fewer are skillful in the use of their tools and applications. Nevertheless in order to develop the mindset for resolving problems, we must grasp a systematic way to identify causation of a problem, and how to implement a corrective action plan for process improvement.

With the information in this book, differentiating with quality can also apply to your personal life. Whether the problem is behavioral, relational, financial, medical or mechanical, you can apply this CREATE Process with its 6-step problem-solving process for time-sensitive root cause analysis, corrective action, and continuous Improvement.

Of course, while we have routines and rituals to keep our days and life flowing on track - we cannot ignore the need for a systemic way to troubleshoot problems when they occur outside of the norm of our routines and rituals. While we know that life is not perfect, and we would like to believe that things will always go right – we need a repeatable process to find and fix problems when things go wrong.

This is where a continuous improvement process would be most helpful. The CREATE Process is one such continuous improvement methodology that gives you the advantage of processing not-so-good news and unfavorable circumstances in life. This doesn't mean that once you become familiar with the CREATE Process that you are expected to have all the answers. Instead you will know if gaps still exist in a proposed solution, and the next steps to keep the project moving towards the solution.

In the next several chapters, you will go into details of the 6 steps of the CREATE Process to create a quality lifestyle.

By the time you have finished reading this book, CREATE A Quality Lifestyle, you would have learned how to analyze root causes, implement corrective action plans, and sustain a culture or lifestyle of continuous improvement. The 6 steps of the CREATE Process described herein provide the framework to guide you through the thought-pattern of understanding the cause of a problem and addressing it with appropriate solutions, timely.

6 STEPS OF THE CREATE PROCESS

E very problem has a solution, and every solution comes from a creative process. Each continuous improvement method has the same goal, which is to resolve the problem, and for the process to regain its previous entitlement – or better. Although each continuous improvement process is different and has a slant towards a critical or useful component, the final outcome is to resolve the problem identified as a project objective.

The purpose of the CREATE Process is to provide a systematic way to resolve a defined problem. This is achieved through the CREATE Process for determining related Root Cause Analysis, Corrective Action, and Continuous Improvement. There is also a focus on the timeliness of investigating and resolving the problem effectively.

The CREATE Process has 6 steps, which help to identify the phase of the process improvement. The CREATE Process is easy to remember as the acronym, C.R.E.A.T.E.:
1. **C** represents, Come to Terms
2. **R** represents, Review the Process
3. **E** represents, Evaluate the Problem
4. **A** represents, Accelerate Customized Solutions
5. **T** represents, Trust Proven Relationships; and
6. **E** also represents, Educate Every Time

You should spend a little time to memorize this term, C.R.E.A.T.E. and the representation of each letter of its acronym. Each of the 6 steps of the C.R.E.A.T.E. Process deals with specific activity within the step, and gives a feeling of progression as you accomplish one step and move on to the next.

The CREATE Process is not only useful for maintaining an existing process, but also for developing and error-proofing a new process and improving process capabilities.

Below, we will outline what the CREATE Process is and what the CREATE Process is not, for further understanding.

- The CREATE Process is NOT:
    - an automated response system.
    - a software with algorithms.
    - mathematically based.
    - a solution prediction.

- The CREATE Process is:
    - a methodology to guide resolution of issues.
    - applicable to various disciplines and industries.
    - a time-sensitive approach to risk mitigation.
    - a specific action-oriented, high-level process.
    - a standard process with 6 simple steps.
    - among the other notable continuous improvement methodologies.

To make your learning experience practical, you should think of a problem, what's wrong, and what's keeping you up at night – as a quality project requiring resolution. As you read through this CREATE Process, you can apply these simple steps to see the progress and impact on your identified project objective.

So, does the CREATE Process apply to every problem? Can it provide guaranteed solutions? I believe that it's a great introduction to continuous improvement and the 'quality lifestyle'. The CREATE Process gives you the focus during each step of the process to resolve personal problems and real-life issues. Wherever you are in resolving a problem, you can apply the CREATE process.

STEP 1
COME TO TERMS

Come to Terms is Step 1 of the C.R.E.A.T.E. Process. You must 'Come to Terms' with the alleged problem as identified until you can prove it to be otherwise. Whether it's a complaint or a concern, this requires you to face the facts and trust the truth revealed from the evidences of the 'problem.'

Some questions for Step 1, Come to Terms:
- Why is this problem now a problem?
- Who are the persons involved in the problem?
- Can you verify that this problem will not resolve on its own?
- What process is this problem a part of?
- What are the consequential impacts of this problem?
- Does the problem get worse with time?
- Who will own the resolution of this problem?

The objective of this first step is to verify the reality of the alleged problem. This means that you must gather as much information with relevant evidence from preliminary research and observation. This information is then compared to the acceptable criteria, which are the rules to help determine the following:
- Accept the alleged problem as True – and continue the investigation; or
- Reject the alleged problem as False – and conclude with the evidence as justification.

A simple problem can be resolved mainly by one person. However, more severe problems will require a team approach for conducting in-depth investigations. You will have to make others, who can genuinely contribute to the resolution, be fully aware (see Step 5, Trust Proven Relationship). Be sure to communicate the significance of the problem for the proper accountability and urgency of all participants.

Of course, you cannot ignore that time has elapsed from the point when the problem was discovered (see chapter on Time-sensitivity to Quality Improvement). While you cannot rush quality, you should not procrastinate any effort that drives progress, timely.

ADDITIONAL INFORMATION:
- **LOGISTICS:** Tools of communication, equipment, resources, meeting place and rhythm, and schedules are all important. Preparation and pre-work make much difference and build momentum during meeting review.
- **AGENDA:** Discuss the topics agreed upon with related questions and answers. This includes status updates from previous meetings, and new problems/business.
- **TEAM ROSTER:** State names of individuals or profession that will participate in the problem resolution. These are active members of the core team, who have specific roles and responsibilities, and limited to participants' attendance.
- **PROBLEM STATEMENT:** State the problem using few words to sufficiently describe the problem and its impact for team's full understanding. Use few sentences to state what is wrong or not acceptable and why this is now a problem.
- **GOAL STATEMENT:** State the goal to be achieved with the agreed-upon objectives. Set expectations for deliverables to have by the end of each meeting.
- **COMMITMENT STATEMENT:** Get commitment needed from participants to support the project while their expertise is required.

Step 1: Come to Terms with the reality that either a problem exists and needs to be resolved, or that the problem is insignificant and is justifiable as being acceptable.

STEP 2
REVIEW THE PROCESS

Reveiw the Process is Step 2 of the C.R.E.A.T.E. Process. This means that someone will have to be familiar with the process of how things work and what causes things not to work. You will have to examine the problem to determine what process was affected. Wherever the problem shows up, by reviewing the process you can help in identifying process gaps, modes of failure, and opportunities for improvement.

Some questions for Step 2, Review the Process:
- Do you know someone who is knowledgeable about the problem or process?
- Where in the process did the problem occur?
- Can sub-processes be isolated to narrow scope of problem?
- Is there documentation that explains this problem or how this part of the process should operate?
- Is the process in its active, static or dynamic state?

Knowing someone who is familiar with the process, or the problem, or is confident in its resolution is valuable. These individuals are called Subject Matter Experts (SMEs). With the little information you provide to them, they in turn can explain a lot in details to you. They are the ones who can provide the expertise in their subject matter to the team to navigate through various decisions.

By design, every solution comes from a creative process. Generally, a process is constructed step by step to produce good outcomes that are acceptable to its users. From the input of raw materials to types of equipment utilized, to the competency of operators, every process is engineered for quality goods, products and services.

Nevertheless no process is perfect. There will always be variations in the process – as designed. Even raw materials will have several minute differences in characteristics, equipment will age, and human errors will be lurking variables over time.

ADDITIONAL INFORMATION:

- SCOPE OF THE PROBLEM: To properly investigate the problem, with the people, time and resources available, it is best to sufficiently scope the problem. These boundaries of the project will maintain focus and drive meaningful discussions.
- SEQUENCE OF EVENTS: Processes can be simplified as steps of activities that produce value through change. Every action or activity should add value in the process.
- RESEARCH SUPPORTIVE FILES: Reference authoritative sources, e.g. Manuals and how-to guides, troubleshooting videos, tutorials, self-help materials and literature, SME advice, and management inputs, and related communications.
- WALK THE TALK: There are many aspects to a process and you should know which one is being reviewed. Oftentimes processes do not operate at their best or ideal conditions. Below are some of the state of a process for your review:
  - The ideal process (aka Perfect),
  - The should-be process (aka Procedural),
  - The believed process (aka Preferred),
  - The actual process (aka Practical), and
  - The neglected process (aka Pitiful).
- DECISION OF PURSUIT: What is the cost and benefit – the so what – of the project to resolve this problem? Do you have a compelling argument to pursue the project?

Step 2: Review the Process and understand how the process should work, and then realize the sequence of events that led to the occurrence of the problem.

STEP 3
EVALUATE THE PROBLEM

E valuate the Problem is Step 3 of the C.R.E.A.T.E. Process. The evaluation of the problem is the Root Cause Analysis (RCA). During the RCA you can ask, Why did the problem and each subsequent reason happen? This is the investigative portion of the project to find what failed in the process and caused the problem.

Some questions for Step 3, Evaluate the Problem:
- Who is the best person to talk with about the problem?
- Why did the problem occur?
- What caused or contributed to the problem?
- Do you have evidence of what caused the problem?
- Can you identify all defective characteristics of the problem?
- Is the causal factor internal or external to the process?

How the problem is defined or expressed can imply the direction of the investigation towards the root cause. You have to replay the scenario, question people involved and check the defect to aid the investigation. Major problems can be divided into sub-projects with different owners.

Again, if from Step 1, Come to Terms, you had concluded that the problem is valid, then you would have gathered objective evidence of its defect. The defect is a characteristic that is typically outside of specification and is not acceptable. This is the flaw of the product called a nonconformance or a discrepancy.

To get to the root cause of a problem, an RCA is required. The first Why response is called the Direct Cause, while the last Why response is called the Root Cause. The direct cause typically relates to people, product, process, or procedure.

Note, the cause of the problem is not the same as the defect of the product. That is why fixing a defect will not eliminate what caused it. It is always easy to replace bad items with good items and keep the process working – but that replacement will be subjected to the existing cause, if the causal factor is not corrected as well.

While all specifics may not be revealed upfront in an investigation or evaluation, significant evidence can be analyzed and interpreted for responsible party to investigate further.

- Direct Cause is the first reason for the nonconformance.
- Root Cause is the final reason for the nonconformance.
- Contributing factor is an enabler to the likelihood of a cause.

ADDITIONAL INFORMATION (FOR ANALYSIS OF THE ROOT CAUSE):

- **RECOGNITION:** Why is this final reason the actual root cause or causal factor?
- **CONFIRMATION:** Does the defective characteristic of the root cause fail the design criteria of the specification?
- **IMPLICATION:** Does optimizing the antithesis of the defective characteristic ensure the prevention of the problem?
- **AUTHORIZATION:** Does the defective characteristic of the problem have traceability to the designer's authorization?

Step 3: Evaluate the Problem such that the result of the root cause analysis will explain the defective characteristic with traceability to the designer's authorization.

STEP 4
ACCELERATE CUSTOMIZED SOLUTIONS

Accelerate Customized Solutions is Step 4 of the C.R.E.A.T.E. Process. The focus of this step is to develop a set of solutions to resolve the problem, the defect and the root cause. That is, to every one problem there will be a set of solutions, including corrections for the problem, the defect and the root cause.

Some questions for Step 4, Accelerate Customized Solutions:
- What immediate actions can be taken to keep unaffected processes functional?
- How can you contain the problem and its consequences?
- What corrective actions can be taken to reactivate the broken process and sustain improvements?
- Do you have the resources to implement corrective actions?
- Who are the owners for each assigned action item?

Remember that every problem has a solution, and every solution comes from a creative process. Do not become intimidated by this creative process to develop useful solutions. This may require some creative thinking but often times the solution already exist in the advanced world – or an alternative replacement can be utilized to make the future process equal or better than the previous process.

Whether you view the problem from a high-level or from a detailed perspective, the set of solutions should correlate and make sense. If the root cause of the problem is not simplified, then the solutions can be confusing. However, when you make the root cause plain and simple, then the solution can be clear – as its antithesis.

You will need documentation of the corrective actions being tracked to completion. This plan of actions includes both short term and long term tasks for the problem-solving process.

- Short Term tasks involve the prior steps: Come to Terms, Review the Process, and Evaluate the Problem. It also includes containing the problem and its consequences.
- Long Term tasks involve this and remaining steps: Accelerate Customized Solution, Trust Proven Relationships, and Educate Every Time. It also includes validating the changes.

What you will be looking for is a plan of action that can show evidence of an improved change. The plan must include something to be done differently for the process to be better. This improved change will also be verified and validated. Too often problems recur from a short-lived solution, so these solutions should withstand and sustain long after the implementation period.

ADDITIONAL INFORMATION:
- **IMMEDIATE ACTIONS:** These actions are done within 48 hours to gather data and initiate a customized team approach.
- **COMMUNICATION:** This documents and notifies key personnel.
- **CONTAINMENT:** This determines the scope of impact by the problem and its consequences on anything else.
- **CORRECTIONS:** These are acceptable changes to what was previously defective.
- **SOLUTION SET:** For every problem there is a set of solutions. The set of solution will include 'fixes' for the problem, defect and root cause. The set of solution will include short term and long term related tasks.

Step 4: Accelerate Customized Solutions and get to the best set of solutions quickly.

.

STEP 5
TRUST PROVEN RELATIONSHIPS

Trust Proven Relationships is Step 5 of the C.R.E.A.T.E. Process. The focus of this step is to assign the work associated with the set of solutions to appropriate owners. Note, the problem is still yet to be solved but by now you have a corrective action plan with various tasks to be completed. You now need to hold actionees and teams accountability to completing these tasks effectively.

Some questions for Step 5, Trust Proven Relationships:
- Do you have approval to make all the changes proposed?
- Do you have persons with appropriate level of skill needed to perform the corrective action tasks?
- Are people committed for the duration of the project?
- Who will monitor the changes as tasks are completed or at risk to become overdue?
- Do the tasks have time-sensitive due dates?
- When is the new process expected to be launched?

For work to actually get done by skillful individuals, professionalism must be demanded. The team must show mutual respect, comply with business ethics and share common values. This makes the working environment open to participation and voluntary thoughts without criticism. You should set ground rules for respecting each person's opinion, space, experience, time, and culture.

Be aware that the team that investigated or evaluated the problem will not necessarily be the team that will physically implement the solutions that correct the problem. You have to now trust the relationships of the team that will make the improved changes.

Many times SMEs who own operate a function will be tasked to implement the improvement. SMEs understand specific functions of work, procedures, and oftentimes the history behind the process.

Problems are solved when people, who own corrective action tasks, complete them as planned. It is necessary to have urgency to fulfill each task's objective. The longer a solution takes to implement, then greater will be the risk to complete it – especially as competing prioritizes may arise requirement their expertise as well.

Sometimes expertise may come from people external to the team, such as a contractor or consultant. As prospects they should be interviewed and screened to determine best fit for team and project involved.

Finally, you should appreciate everyone on the team, especially those who specialize in certain fields, who hold years of experience, and who are certified to bring a level of trust and expertise. Without the individual contributor the overall project would not succeed.

ADDITIONAL INFORMATION:
- **ROLES AND RESPONSIBILITY:** Unless the role and responsibility of each team member is defined or is known by all, then you will have to facilitate the initial performance of the team.
- **ACCOUNTABILITY:** Once an individual accepts the responsibility to participate within the team, she will have to onus to complete her related task.
- **TASK IMPACT:** Each task will have a different level of impact on the overall improvement. Tasks can be weighted to indicate the simplicity and impact to overall objective.
- **EVIDENCE OF CHANGE:** There must be a change with eveidence. It must affect the fit, form, feature or function of the existing process. The problem will not improve by itself - without the change. You need to compare the before and after states to verify the actual change.

Step 5: Trust Proven Relationships and assign qualified individuals to be trusted for completing corrective action items, on-time.

STEP 6
EDUCATE EVERY TIME

E ducate Every Time is Step 6 of the C.R.E.A.T.E. Process. The focus of this step is to become sufficiently knowledgeable to communicate what has been done. Many times getting the knowledge is the first step of a typical process, but it is the last step of this process, which allows educate with some experience.

Some questions for Step 6, Educate Every Time:
- Has each individual responsible for a task confirmed that the task is done?
- Who is responsible for all documents received?
- Who will provide training for users of the new process?
- Who will audit the process to verify that the new process has sustained expectations with its first year?
- What will be your customer feedback mechanism?

Oftentimes your age, interest, background, experience, exposure and field of study do help to deal with problems differently from your peers, who are faced with similar issues. The reality is that exercising the knowledge of this CREATE Process will empower you to make better informed decisions. This will increase your level of awareness and cognitive skill to pay closer attention to details.

Having a known solution for a known problem can be beneficial to many people if communicated. This process improvement should be communicated for people to know the changes incorporated. This is a part of your best practice and lesson-learn experience.

By now in the CREATE Process, you will be able to analyze problems and follow any improvement efforts for your personal growth and development. You can revisit projects for continuous improvement and demonstrate a quality lifestyle by doing the following:
- Share knowledge with others.

- Attend informational courses, social events, and seminars.
- Subscribe to reliable sources, and organizations.
- Participate in problem-solving, and robust solution efforts.

You now have the knowledge to lead or facilitate a team through the CREATE Process. You are knowledgeable to explain the steps of the CREATE Process. Whether it's conducting a root cause analysis, implementing a set of solutions with corrective actions, or advancing through incremental changes through continuous improvement efforts, you are equipped as a problem solver. You can instruct anyone step-by-step how to create a quality lifestyle.

ADDITIONAL INFORMATION:
- **ENCOURAGEMENT:** Your solution can encourage someone else. This has provided you with experience to help someone else.
- **WORDS OF WISDOM:** You have a wealth of information to share. Self edification helps to understand the changes that occurred. Share your testimony within your community.
- **FORMAL REPORTS:** Documenting the findings and the final results of a project will help everyone to understand the new process and changes. Storage and retrieval of the documentation of your projects will help future projects.
- **CUSTOMER SATISFACTION:** The result of the CREATE Process will satisfy customers and delight people who benefit from the outcome. Customer enjoy when problem are truly solved.

Step 6: Educate Every Time and take the time to educate yourself and inform others of the quality improvements.

TIME–SENSITIVITY TO QUALITY IMPROVEMENT

Time management is important to a quality lifestyle. We have to work while we have the time, and since problems are not a part of the plan, we have less time to resolve it and continue to work. Having sensitivity to time is important during the process improvement efforts. The longer it takes to resolve a problem, the more costly and devastating the consequences can become. When a process is hampered by a problem it can produce defective products or stop the work until all issues are resolved.

Not all problems have a high level of difficulty or uncertainty. Some problems are easier to solve than others and so their resolution cycle times are much shorter – if there is no procrastination.

Below are times associated with events of a typical problem:
- **TIME OF ACTUAL DEFECT OCCURRENCE:** Oftentimes when a defect occurs it goes unnoticed for a while. It can be a considerable amount of time before someone actually discovers that an unintentional defect has occurred.
- **TIME OF ACTUAL PROBLEM OBSERVANCE:** This is normally the easiest and quickest way to recognize a existence of a discrepancy. The problem is usually something that is out of the norm to the observant eye.
- **TIME OF ACTUAL DEFECT DISCOVERY:** This is the point in time when there is verification that the defective characteristic is not compliant with the requirements of the specifications. If other products are suspected to have same defect, a list of effectivity should be compiled and containment should be communicated and completed. (Note, this time at which the defect is discovered is different from the time when the defect actually had occurred.)
- **TIME OF ACTUAL DEFECT CORRECTION:** Correction of the problem – or rather the defect – can be completed normally by a

rework or a replacement with a conforming part – provided that the problem no longer exists. If the problem still exists, then the replacement part will also succumb to the defect.

- **TIME OF ACTUAL ROOT CAUSE ANALYSIS:** This goes to the point in time where the team determines the source of what created and caused the defect.
- **TIME OF ACTUAL CORRECTIVE ACTIONS:** This is the point in time where the a set of solutions is listed and sources of error are corrected, and prevented from changing without detection.
- **TIME OF ACTUAL IMPROVEMENT VERIFICATION:** After all the improvements have been made, this is the time where a product goes through the renewed and changed process to verify that the improvement actually works.
- **TIME OF ACTUAL RENEWED PROCESS ENTITLEMENT:** This is the point in time where the benefits of the new process is recognized and usually handed over to the functional team.

The time-sensitivity to quality improvement does not have to wait for a specific date to be completed. Whether it is an action related to root cause, corrective action or continuous improvement, you need to complete the assignment sooner than later to gain the benefit of the improvement. The quicker the process can continue to produce acceptable and conforming products, or can be error-proofed, then the better.

Just imagine a product with a defect earlier in its process that goes through several 'value-added' steps only to be scrapped as waste!

You can have a great process, but if it takes forever to complete each task or if there is procrastination, then the less effective that process improvement effort will be. Since there is always another project pending, time management is critical for improvement. This time-sensitivity to quality improvement efforts takes resources, skills, integrity and cooperation to be effective.

BENEFITS OF A QUALITY LIFESTYLE

A manufacturing manager once asked me the meaning of the statement in my email signature, "Differentiating With Quality". Being sensitive to his query – and aware that Manufacturing actually makes the products and not Quality – I replied, "Many people and organization focus on their particular criteria such as Cost, Thru-put, Sales, Delivery, Safety but customers generally experience the Quality of the product or service provided to them and their consumers.

Here, **#DifferentiatingWithQuality** means that you can outperform your competitors by meeting all customer criteria with quality.

A QUALITY LIFESTYLE IS NOVEL
Oftentimes the problem requiring your immediate attention is a 'new issue' – to you. Once the problem is realized, the underlying defect may or may not be known and the related causes must be determined. This means you have to gear-up confidence for the gradient of the learning curve when such a problem arises.

Note, there is no need to feel intimidated by the unknown project at hand. You have the CREATE Process with a team to support you throughout the problem-solving methodology.

A QUALITY LIFESTYLE IS CHALLENGING
Whether it's a year-over-year productivity goal or a new challenge, the quality lifestyle has its obstacles and hindrances to overcome and pitfalls to avoid. With a toolbox of process methodologies, drawers of process tools and a disciplined mindset, you can face any challenge and scope the problem in a logical manner and proceed through each step and solve it in a systematical way.

You will have to work with people of various mindsets and attitudes. However, the more you become familiar with this comprehensive method and its 6-step problem-solving process for root cause, correct action, and continuous improvement, then the greater the impact and easier, less stressful and frustrating the project will be.

A QUALITY LIFESTYLE IS GOAL-ORIENTED
So with a focus to go through the CREATE Process, you will see purpose towards being goal-oriented to fulfilling objectives and assigned activities. Each step has its deliverables and outcome, and leads into the next step. It's important to set expectations of meaningful deliverables at the end of every meeting.

The goal statement should be a short and simple sentence defining the desired outcome from the onset of the project. Subsequently, a set of objectives and action items and related tasks will support the goal statement for assigned individuals to be responsible for accomplishing each task.

Otherwise, if an objective, action item or task is not critical to achieving your goal, then it should be reconsidered for elimination so that full effort and resource is reassigned accordingly.

A QUALITY LIFESTYLE IS HARD-WORK
It takes hard-work and perseverance to be a change-agent. It takes hard-work to diligently follow the CREATE Process with its 6-step problem-solving methodology. It may require pre-work, ground work, homework, rework and follow-up to see things happen. No doubt, a quality lifestyle requires work.

This ensures there are no significant gaps that can adversely affect the project's outcome. Hard-work, smart-work and consistency in making the calls, scheduling meetings, facilitating discussions through conflicts, influencing stakeholders and controllers, and steering the diversely opinionated team.

A QUALITY LIFESTYLE IS EMOTIONAL

Any person with a clean heart and a right spirit for excellence will get emotional at some point in a project that really matters. So it is also for SMEs, who take their work seriously and always to heart. When emotions are deeply seated and thoughts are shared openly there can be heated discussions and flares of temper tantrums.

Nevertheless, most people care about their jobs. As process owners, and SMEs they know the effect of change imposed on their daily work lives once implemented and adapted procedurally. Once their business procedures and work instructions are revised with changes incorporated, then their typical signatures or approvals must adhere to the inherent change of the updated process.

Please approach emotional issues with caution. Be forgiving. Listen with ears and heart and most of all be professional in verbal and non-verbal, body languages.

A QUALITY LIFESTYLE IS PRACTICAL

There are usually few tools that are applicable to each step and should be leveraged to document outcome. The result is change – visual change – to fit, form, feature, and/or function of a hardware or software. This should be obvious when there is a side-by-side comparison such as a 'Before and After' views, respectively.

The visual management of change implemented is practical and critically important in verifying the effort of the root cause analysis and corrective actions. You cannot complete any continuous improvement project without the evidence of a change, whether from a high-level or detailed level review. There must be a notable change in fit, form, feature, or function within the process, goods, products, or service.

A QUALITY LIFESTYLE IS MATURING

Whether you are a certified, qualified or beginner quality personnel, you are deemed to grow and mature in the discipline of Quality

Assurance once you adapt the quality lifestyle to your daily thought life and routine practices.

The selection of proper usage of problem-solving methodologies, the tools and techniques are fundamental to your skill-set development and effective communication of process steps. This is similar to a workman who is skillful in determining the correct tool for a particular task.

A Quality Lifestyle is Transitional

The exposure, the training, and the tools you use during your quality lifestyle develop critical thinking and transferable skills. You can use them in your personal lives as well as in an organization. Although projects may have different scenarios and details, you may be able to reuse some tools, if applicable.

The quality lifestyle is transitional. There is always another new project with significant business impact or concern requiring your attention – whether as a project leader, facilitator, coach or individual contributor. At the end of each project, be ready to transfer process and project ownership to appropriate persons with the necessary overlapping training on process and documentation.

Note, recurring problems are never welcomed and always require fine-tuning and optimization of process controls to account for gaps in project scope and oversight in corrective measures' sustainability. Oftentimes, these gaps may arise when there are new persons, suppliers, equipment, products, techniques and procedures being introduced to the process.

A Quality Lifestyle is Rewarding

There is a great reward in achieving your assignment on a Quality Lifestyle project. There is reward in delighting a customer whether internal or external and whether directly or indirectly. There is reward in personal growth and development as you learn and become familiar with new process, product, procedure and people.

The impact of applying the knowledge and working with a team on the CREATE Process have significant benefits to you as an individual, and your organization both financially and educationally.

PURSUING A QUALITY INITIATIVE
I applaud you for taking this quality initiative by first learning this novel quality methodology, called the CREATE Process. CREATE is easy to remember as the 6-step problem-solving process that was developed to benefit you. C.R.E.A.T.E. is an acronym meaning:
- ✓ **C**ome to Terms
- ✓ **R**eview the Process
- ✓ **E**valuate the Problem
- ✓ **A**ccelerate Customized Solutions
- ✓ **T**rust Proven Relationships
- ✓ **E**ducate Every Time

Sure there are unique challenges to face. However, this CREATE Process will supplement your knowledge and guide you through the 6 steps progressively as you seek to maintain a quality of life through personal growth and development. Stay true to original intents of quality control, quality assurance and continuous improvement methodologies. Always emphasize the importance of innovation and creativity to investigate and resolve real-life issues.

SUMMARY – A QUALITY LIFESTYLE
The key prerequisite to embodying the Quality Lifestyle is to be open-minded and respectful by having a clean heart and the right spirit as you interact with people for the betterment. Whether you need to create a solution for improving an existing process or for developing a new process, this CREATE Process will help the everyday person like you with a simple 6-step problem-solving process for time-sensitive root cause analysis, corrective action, and continuous improvement to managing personal problems and improving real-life issues.

CONCLUSION

"Every problem has a solution, and every solution comes from a creative process." – Sir Rob Reid

You can create a quality lifestyle by consistently applying this C.R.E.A.T.E. Process to resolve or eliminate real life issues. When you are faced with major decisions or life events that can significantly alter your future, family, finance and faith, you will need a systematic methodology to guide your thoughts and actions.

Every problem has a solution, and every solution comes from a creative process. The CREATE Process is an easy-to-remember 6-step problem-solving process for time-sensitive Root Cause Analysis, Corrective Action, and Continuous Improvement. In six simple steps you can have a clear and concrete mindset that focuses on systematical way of excellence and drives the discipline of a quality lifestyle. The C.R.E.A.T.E. Process entails:

1. **C**ome to Terms
2. **R**eview the Process
3. **E**valuate the Problem
4. **A**ccelerate Customized Solutions
5. **T**rust Proven Relationships
6. **E**ducate Every Time

It is good to have a controlled process to keep things on track. It is even better to also have a contingency plan in the event that things get off-track. Just like having a dentist or a mechanic, think of me as your Quality Leader guiding you through the CREATE Process as your contingency plan – there to help you to get back on-track and in control after things have gone wrong.

With these steps, I want you to win in life and succeed at what you do – even in tough times. I want you to overcome every obstacle and achieve your goals despite adversities. So don't get stuck and don't ever give up on your hopes and dreams. Get to the best set of solutions quickly by using the systematic approach of the above CREATE Process!

I can almost guarantee that every poor decision or wrongful action will be predicated on a step within the CREATE Process that was inadvertently overlooked or intentionally ignored. Even if the responsibility of solving a problem was deferred to someone else, you can still follow along and track the choices by referencing the CREATE Process to justify the results.

Whether the problem is behavioral, relational, financial, medical or mechanical, you can apply this CREATE Process.

If you want peace of mind, and a quality of life, then you should apply the steps of the CREATE Process. Let this CREATE Process guide you through each step of the problem-solving process progressively. You can achieve personal growth and development once you decide to create a quality lifestyle.

APPENDIX

APPENDIX A
DEFINITIONS OF QUALITY

DEFINITION OF QUALITY BY AMERICAN SOCIETY FOR QUALITY (ASQ)
Quality of defined as a subjective term for which each person or sector has its own definition. In technical usage, quality can have two meanings:
1. The characteristics of a product or service that bear on its ability to satisfy stated or implied needs;
2. A product or service free of deficiencies.

DEFINITION OF QUALITY BY MERRIAM-WEBSTER DICTIONARY
plural qualities
1. a: peculiar and essential character: nature
2. a degree of excellence
3. a: social status
4. a: distinguishing attribute
5. the character in a logical proposition of being affirmative or negative
6. vividness of hue
7. a: timbre
8. the attribute of an elementary sensation that makes it fundamentally unlike any other sensation

DEFINITION OF QUALITY MANAGEMENT BY INTERNATIONAL ORGANIZATION FOR STANDARDIZATION (ISO)
ISO 9001 is a standard that sets out the requirements for a quality management system. It helps businesses and organizations to be more efficient and improve customer satisfaction.

A quality management system is a way of defining how an organization can meet the requirements of its customers and other stakeholders affected by its work.

APPENDIX B
QUALITY QUOTES

I. CREATE a Quality Lifestyle. **– Rob Reid**
II. Quality is a set of criteria for customer satisfaction. **– Rob Reid**
III. Differentiating with Quality. **– Rob Reid**
IV. Every problem has a solution, and every solution comes from a creative process. **– Rob Reid**

1. Assignable causes of variation may be found and eliminated. **– Walter Shewhart**
2. Quality is everyone's responsibility. **– W Edwards Deming**
3. Quality means doing it right when no one is looking. **– Henry Ford**
4. Without a standard there is no logical basis for making a decision or taking action. **– Joseph Juran**
5. Quality has to be caused, not controlled. **– Philip Crobsy**
6. Quality Control starts and ends with training. **– Kaoru Ishikawa**
7. Quality is never an accident; it is always the result of intelligent effort. **– John Ruskin**
8. Quality is remembered long after the price is forgotten. **– Ed Sabol**
9. Quality Is not an act, it is a habit. **– Aristotle**
10. Techniques don't produce Quality products and services; people do, people who care, people who are treated as creatively contributing individuals. **– Tom Peters**
11. Be a yardstick of Quality. Some people aren't used to an environment where excellence is expected. **– Steve Jobs**
12. The Quality of your work, in the long run, is the deciding factor on how much your services are valued by the world. **– Orison Swett Marden**
13. It is the quality of our work which will please God and not the quantity. **– Mahatma Gandhi**
14. Quality in a service or product is not what you put into it. It is what the customer gets out of it. **– Peter Drucker**
15. Quality is an investment in the future. **– Unknown**

16. Quality isn't expensive, it's priceless. **– Unknown**
17. Speed, Price, Quality: Pick Two. **– The Economist**
18. Excellence is the unlimited ability to improve the Quality of what you have to offer. **– Rick Pitino**
19. Quality questions create a quality life. Successful people ask better questions, and as a result, they get better answers. **– Anthony Robbins**
20. Success is a process, a Quality of mind and way of being, an outgoing affirmation of life. **– Alex Noble**
21. Quality begins on the inside... and then works its way out. **– Bob Moawad**
22. Quality leads! It is the difference between being average or being number one! **– Unknown**
23. Quality is the best business plan. **– John Lasseter**
24. The Quality of our work depends on the Quality of our people. **– Unknown**
25. Quality first! Every day, every hour, every second, it's giving your best, every time, all the time. **– Unknown**
26. Quality means "fitness for use." **– Joseph Juran**
27. "Conformance to requirements." **– Philip Crosby**

APPENDIX C
QUALITY TOOLS

No matter which methodology you choose for creating a culture of problem-solving, they all utilize formal tools and graphical techniques to hone creativity and harness solutions. Tools are a workman's best friend for getting a job done correctly and consistently. These quality tools provide the guidance and triggers the input/output expected to comprehend and conclude specific issues. With this said, it is critical to choose the appropriate tool to manage the information to be provided and to meet the deliverable to be produced.

PROBLEM-SOLVING TOOLS FOR THE CREATE PROCESS

These are some of the quality tools that you can become familiar with to help guide a process for continuous improvement. Each tool can be used in the CREATE Process step listed.

QUALITY TOOLS – COME TO TERMS
- ✓ Voice of Customer (Feedback)
- ✓ S.M.A.R.T. Goals
- ✓ Team Charter

QUALITY TOOLS – REVIEW THE PROCESS
- ✓ Process Map or Flow Chart
- ✓ Sequence of Events
- ✓ Drill-down Tree Diagram
- ✓ SIPOC Diagram

QUALITY TOOLS – EVALUATE THE PROBLEM
- ✓ Failure Mode and Effect Analysis (FMEA)
- ✓ 5 Whys (One-legged, Three Legged)
- ✓ Checklist Questionnaire
- ✓ Process of Elimination

QUALITY TOOLS – ACCELERATE CUSTOMIZED SOLUTIONS
- ✓ Benchmark
- ✓ Quality Function Deployment (QFD)
- ✓ Trial and Error Method
- ✓ TRIZ
- ✓ Survey

QUALITY TOOLS – TRUST PROVEN RELATIONSHIPS
- ✓ Contract Agreement
- ✓ License or Permit
- ✓ ARMI or RACI Project Team
- ✓ NDA or NCA
- ✓ Action Item List (AIL)

QUALITY TOOLS – EDUCATE EVERY TIME
- ✓ Meeting Minutes
- ✓ Training and Presentation
- ✓ Alerts and Notifications
- ✓ Metrics and Reports

THE SEVEN BASIC TOOLS OF QUALITY
Also called Seven Classic Tools of Quality, they are the graphical techniques often used to resolve quality related issues with little training. These basic quality tools are as follows:
- ✓ Cause and Effect Diagram (Fishbone or Ishikawa Diagram)
- ✓ Check Sheet
- ✓ Control Chart
- ✓ Histogram
- ✓ Pareto Chart
- ✓ Scatter Diagram
- ✓ Stratification (Flow Chart, Run Chart)

APPENDIX D
CAREERS IN QUALITY

All levels are experience within Quality organization can benefit from learning this CREATE Process to help guide them through the 6-step problem-solving process for root cause analysis, corrective action and continuous improvement. Whether as an individual new to Quality position or a seasoned veteran in Quality Management, this CREATE Process provides the mental framework and procedural disciplined mindset to achieve the goal and objectives of your quality project.

INSPECTOR: Inspects, audits, and report on materials, processes, and products using measuring instruments and techniques to ensure conformance with an organization's specification. Inspector's work follows the mechanic's work, which he inspects and audits.

CALIBRATION TECHNICIAN: Tests, calibrates, maintains, and repairs various measuring instruments, and equipment, which inspectors and mechanics utilize. Also initiates out of tolerance reports.

ANALYST: Gathers, analyzes and presents quality-related data from business operations activities using statistical techniques to drive business decisions.

QUALITY ENGINEER: Designs, implements, and evaluates quality assurance processes and procedures for compliance with standards and policies. Provides responses to customer corrective action requests to resolve findings. Interacts with other business functions within an organization and with customers and suppliers representatives on quality-related issues.

SIX SIGMA BLACK BELT: Implements process improvement projects, trains and mentors Green Belts in the organization to increase business productivity and customer satisfaction.

Auditor: Performs audit on business practices, and reports on compliance to quality system performance.

Quality Assurance Supervisor: Guides daily decisions for staff members, such as inspectors who reports to her. Approves team's workload, travel requirements and weekly timesheets.

Quality Manager: Ensures proper staffing, and adequacy of resources. Represents organization as SME on quality related issues. Provides quality business direction and input to upper management. Creates and revises quality documents within the Quality Management System.

ROBERT A. REID

www.ingramcontent.com/pod-product-compliance
Lightning Source LLC
Chambersburg PA
CBHW051405280526
45784CB00007B/3102